Anthology for the Earth

First U.S. edition 1998

Library of Congress Cataloging-in-Publication Data
Anthology for the earth / collected by Judy Allen. — 1st U.S. ed.
Summary: An illustrated anthology of poetry and prose about the natural world,
by such authors as Rudyard Kipling, Ovid, and Tolstoy.
ISBN 0-7636-0301-5
1. Nature—Literary collections. [1. Nature—Literary collections.] I. Allen, Judy.
PZ5.A593   1998
808.8'036—dc21   97-674

2 4 6 8 10 9 7 5 3 1

Printed in Belgium

Candlewick Press
2067 Massachusetts Avenue
Cambridge, Massachusetts 02140

Anthology for the Earth

Edited by Judy Allen

CANDLEWICK PRESS
CAMBRIDGE, MASSACHUSETTS

Contents

INTRODUCTION

*F*or me, the best thing about this book—
apart from the fact that it looks so beautiful—is that everyone who has worked on it loves it.
And that's exactly *why* it's so beautiful. Every painting, every drawing, shows the powerful
reaction of the artist to the words illustrated—a reaction which is often dramatic,
sometimes affectionate, always passionate.
This anthology started in my early teens when I was given a stout hardcover notebook.
In it I copied out extracts and poems about the natural world that seemed to me
important, special, magical.
The pieces I chose said things I already believed but had been unable to express.
Some confirmed how extraordinary and complex and generous and beautiful the world is;
some were inspired by pain and rage at the needless damage we've inflicted on it;
others showed that it doesn't have to be like this. They were statements to live by—
messages from the wise—warning notices and useful signposts.
Reading them again, so many years later, was a surprisingly emotional experience.
The writers were people whose work I still respect and admire. Their words affected me as
strongly as they had when I was young. They made me want to add more recent discoveries
and to hunt around in libraries for half-forgotten poems, half-remembered statements of belief.
Now that a selection of these pieces is published, illuminated by such varied images,
I can see that everything here, words and pictures, is both personal and universal.
Strong magic indeed!

Judy Allen

In the Museum
of Past Centuries

WE HAVE

ELEPHANT TUSKS,
  A GRAY SEAL
THE SONGS OF
  A BLUE WHALE,
WHITE SNOW,
  GREEN FIELDS,
THE RAIN FOREST'S
  VERY LAST TREE.

IN THE MUSEUM
OF PAST CENTURIES
WE HAVE

ENGLISH WOLVES,
DODO BIRDS,
AZTECS, INCAS,
TASMANIAN ABORIGINES.

IN THE MUSEUM
OF PAST CENTURIES
WE HAVE

STINKING RIVERS,
ACID LAKES,
DYING FISH,
DEAD SEAS.

IN THE MUSEUM
OF PAST CENTURIES
WE HAVE

MUSTARD GAS,
BARBED WIRE,
ATOM BOMBS,
A LEAD CONTAINER
MARKED "DEADLY."

IN THE MUSEUM
OF PAST CENTURIES
WE HAVE

(STANDING ALONE)
A SINGLE GLASS CASE,
INSIDE, AN APPLE
THAT'S BEEN BITTEN TWICE:
OLD, TEMPTING, AND JUICY.

KEVIN McCANN

The natural world is not static, nor has it ever been. Forests have turned into grassland, savannahs have become deserts, estuaries have silted up and become marshes, ice caps have advanced and retreated. Rapid though these changes have been, seen in the perspective of geological history, animals and plants have been able to respond to them and so maintain a continuity of fertility almost everywhere. But man is now imposing such swift changes that organisms seldom have time to adapt to them. And the scale of our changes is now gigantic. We are so skilled in our engineering, so inventive with chemicals, that we can, in a few months, transform not merely a stretch of a stream or a corner of a wood, but a whole river system, an entire forest. . . .

As far as we can tell, our planet is the only place in all the black immensities of the universe where life exists. We are alone in space. And the continued existence of life now rests in our hands.

DAVID ATTENBOROUGH FROM THE LIVING PLANET

IF WE DO NOT FAITHFULLY PERFORM, EVERY MORNING AT DAYBREAK, THESE CEREMONIES WE HAVE BEEN GIVEN BY OUR GRANDFATHERS, WE BELIEVE THAT THE SUN WILL NOT RISE AND THE RAINS WILL NOT COME. WE DO THEM SO THAT OUR PEOPLE — AND NOT ONLY OUR PEOPLE — MAY BE FED AND LIVE. LIFE ITSELF DEPENDS ON A CONNECTION WITH THE GREAT SPIRIT; WE TRY TO KEEP THAT CONNECTION OPEN IN THIS WAY. IF WE DO NOT DO THIS, NOT EVEN THE GREAT SPIRIT CAN REACH US, AND THROUGH US OUR MOTHER EARTH. Look what you people are doing to Her! In my nation's territory, coal and uranium are being ripped from the earth, leaving huge wounds. The tailings of plutonium from bomb production poison Rocky Flats. Not even our sacred sites are spared. Diseases spread among our people and many children are born dead or so damaged we wish they were dead. But the worst is that we are even forgetting our own ceremonies, and few of us now hear and experience the movement of the Spirit within us that our ceremonies allow us to receive. Your people have forgotten altogether and lost what your traditions, in the beginning, had established also in you. But some of you are searching, and we will therefore help you to find the Red Road once again, if you will listen to us. But I fear that, as our prophecies have foretold, you will not be able to hear. In that case, destruction will indeed befall us all, and this earth, once so alive and pure and bountiful, will wither and die, murdered by unconscious human insanity.

JAMES GEORGE QUOTING GRANDFATHER DAVID, CHIEF OF THE HOPI NATION, FROM ASKING FOR THE EARTH

The adoption of the Radical Change Scenario, which is the only one that can possibly save our planet, means that each one of us has to take total responsibility for all our actions, without even asking ourselves whether our own tiny contribution will make any difference or not. We are not responsible for what other people do, and, except by example and persuasion, we cannot influence them. But we are responsible for what we do. We may or may not believe that we are to be held responsible for our actions in our lives, that we

are to be held in some way accountable, but we must believe (because we all know it in our hearts, which is really the only way we can know anything) that Nature, or God, or the Life Force—but something, call it what you will—has fitted each one of us with a thing we call a conscience; and it is that that will reward us, or punish us, according to our deserts. We make our own Heaven or Hell.

JOHN SEYMOUR FROM
LIVING AS THOUGH THE WORLD MATTERED

15

*I*n the old days, when a Seneca had located medicinal herbs

that he wished to gather, he would first build a small fire.

After the flames had died, he would throw a pinch of tobacco on the

embers, praying, "I will not destroy you but plant your seeds

that you may come again and yield fourfold more." Then he would dig

the plants, break off the seed stalks, and drop the pods into the hole,

gently covering them with leaf mold, saying, "The plant

will come again, and I have not destroyed life but helped increase it."

❧

*W*hether the Seneca gatherer had actually increased the plant stock

would depend upon a number of factors. . . . What can be

said with certainty is that the man had increased the cost to himself.

Moreover, one would not gather herbs indiscriminately

if a time-consuming ritual such as this were required in every case.

JOHN BIERHORST FROM THE WAY OF THE EARTH

HARVEST HYMN

We spray the field and scatter
   the poison on the ground
So that no wicked wild flowers
   Upon our farm be found.
We like whatever helps us
   To line our purse with pence;
The Twenty-four-hour broiler-house
   And neat electric fence.

All concrete sheds around us
   And Jaguars in the yard,
The telly lounge and deep-freeze
   Are ours from working hard.

We fire the fields for harvest,
   The hedges swell with flame,
The oak trees and the cottages
   From which our grandfathers came.
We give no compensation,
   The earth is ours today,
And if we lose on arable,
   Then bungalows will pay.

All concrete sheds around us
   And Jaguars in the yard,
The telly lounge and deep-freeze
   Are ours from working hard.

JOHN BETJEMAN

Aunty Jean used to come down and stay with me. . . . Her hair was that red I'd say to her, "Aunty, what's the matter with your hair. You been dyeing it?" "No," she'd say, "it's the iron ore. It's all over everything."

That's the mining that did that, all that tearing up of the earth to get to minerals. When they first talked about getting the iron ore and putting it on Finucane Island, the Aborigines up there were very upset. That island was a ceremonial ground; it was only five hundred yards across from the mainland, so when the tide went out those Aborigines would go there to have their rituals.

I was up there when that iron ore first started, when they started loading it onto the boats, and the dust kicked up was terrible. It was really red and it blew from west to east, all over the port. Hedland used to be such a beautiful town but it's ruined now.

Even when they could see how the dust was choking the place they didn't stop; they just kept on going. They even tried putting hoses and sprinklers to stop it from blowing around but it didn't work. When I used to come in from Hillside I couldn't believe it; everything you touched was red. Even the poinciana trees lost their beauty, and they used to be the pride of Port Hedland when they were flowering.

All that mining and destroying of the land is something that worries me a lot. It's not only happening in the Pilbara either; it's everywhere. The world is off its axis. They're destroying everything just to make money.

To me, Australia is a big country, and it's crying poverty today, all through people being greedy.

ALICE NANNUP FROM WHEN THE PELICAN LAUGHED

Greed is
the real dirt,
not dust.

BUDDHIST SCRIPTURES

THE DEVELOPER

The dust of the developer is blown about the field;
Greed and bad faith both fed the flame,
Manipulation's mangle broke his blackened bones
And cynicism swept him up to throw him all away.
His concrete crumbles and his timbers fall;
Tree roots are gently heaving at his last brick wall.

Persistent gentleness has made his tarmac yield,
A garden growing in a road that's lost his name.
His builder's artefacts break down to earth and stones,
Sun, rain, and frost reducing, day by day.
His millions melted, lost beyond recall:
The man's a monument! Example to us all!

ANTHONY DUNCAN

What difference does it make if some species are extinguished, if even half of all the species on earth disappear?

Let me count the ways. . . . Still undeveloped medicines, crops, pharmaceuticals, timber, fibers, pulp, soil-restoring vegetation, petroleum substitutes, and other products and amenities will never come to light.
It is fashionable in some quarters to wave aside the small and obscure, the bugs and weeds, forgetting that an obscure moth from Latin America saved Australia's pastureland from overgrowth by cactus, that the rosy periwinkle provided the cure for Hodgkin's disease and childhood lymphocytic leukemia, that the bark of the Pacific yew offers hope for victims of ovarian and breast cancer, that a chemical from the saliva of leeches dissolves blood clots during surgery, and so on down a roster already grown long and illustrious despite the limited research addressed to it.

I do not mean to suggest that every ecosystem now be viewed as a factory of useful products. Wilderness has a virtue unto itself and needs no extraneous justification.

EDWARD O. WILSON FROM THE DIVERSITY OF LIFE

24

EXTINCTIONS, OF COURSE, HAVE BEEN HAPPENING FOR MILLIONS OF YEARS: ANIMALS AND PLANTS WERE DISAPPEARING LONG BEFORE PEOPLE ARRIVED ON THE SCENE. BUT WHAT HAS CHANGED IS THE EXTINCTION *RATE*.

For millions of years, on average, one species became extinct every century. But most of the extinctions since prehistoric times have occurred in the last three hundred years.

And most of the extinctions that have occurred in the last three hundred years have occurred in the last fifty.

And most of the extinctions that have occurred in the last fifty have occurred in the last ten.

It is the sheer rate of acceleration that is as terrifying as anything else. There are now more than a thousand different species of animals and plants becoming extinct every year.

There are currently five billion human beings and our numbers are continually growing. We are fighting for space with the world's wildlife, which has to contend with hunting, pollution, pesticides, and, most important of all, the loss of habitat. . . .

But . . . does it really matter if the Yangtze river dolphin, or the kakapo, or the northern white rhino, or any other species live on only in scientists' notebooks? Well, yes, it does. Every animal and plant is an integral part of its environment: even Komodo dragons have a major role to play in maintaining the ecological stability of their delicate island homes. If they disappear, so could many other species. And conservation is very much in tune with our own survival. Animals and plants provide us with life-saving drugs and food, they pollinate crops and provide important ingredients for many industrial processes. Ironically, it is often not the big and beautiful creatures, but the ugly and less dramatic ones, that we need most. . . .

There is one last reason for caring, and I believe that no other is necessary. It is certainly the reason why so many people have devoted their lives to protecting the likes of rhinos, parakeets, kakapos, and dolphins. And it is simply this: the world would be a poorer, darker, lonelier place without them.

MARK CARWARDINE FROM LAST CHANCE TO SEE

26

THE AYE-AYE IS A NOCTURNAL LEMUR.

IT IS A VERY STRANGE-LOOKING CREATURE THAT SEEMS TO HAVE BEEN ASSEMBLED FROM BITS OF OTHER ANIMALS. It looks a little like a large cat with a bat's ears, a beaver's teeth, a tail like a large ostrich feather, a middle finger like a long dead twig, and enormous eyes that seem to peer past you into a totally different world which exists just over your left shoulder.

Like virtually everything that lives on Madagascar, it does not exist anywhere else on earth. Its origins date back to a period in earth's history when Madagascar was still part of mainland Africa (which itself had been part of the gigantic supercontinent of Gondwanaland), at which time the ancestors of the Madagascan lemurs were the dominant primate in all the world. When Madagascar sheered off into the Indian Ocean, it became entirely isolated from all the evolutionary changes that took place in the rest of the world. It is a life raft from a different time. It is now almost like a tiny, fragile, separate planet.

The major evolutionary change that passed Madagascar by was the arrival of the monkeys. These were descended from the same ancestors as the lemurs, but they had bigger brains, and were aggressive competitors for the same habitat. Where the lemurs had been content to hang around in trees having a good time, the monkeys were ambitious, and interested in all sorts of things, especially twigs, with which they found they could do all kinds of things that they couldn't do by themselves—dig for things, probe things, hit things. The monkeys took over the world and the lemur branch of the primate family died out everywhere—other than on Madagascar, which for millions of years the monkeys never reached.

Then fifteen hundred years ago, the monkeys finally arrived, or at least the monkey's descendants—us. Thanks to astounding advances in twig technology, we arrived in canoes, then boats, and finally airplanes, and once again started to compete for use of the same habitat, only this time with fire and machetes and domesticated animals, with asphalt and concrete. The lemurs are once again fighting for survival.

DOUGLAS ADAMS FROM LAST CHANCE TO SEE

IT WAS THE INDIAN MANNER TO VANISH INTO THE LANDSCAPE, NOT TO STAND OUT AGAINST IT.

In the working of silver or drilling of turquoise the Indians had exhaustless patience. . . . But their conception of decoration did not extend to the landscape. They seemed to have none of the European's desire to "master" nature, to arrange and re-create. . . . It was as if the great country were asleep, and they wished to carry on their lives without awakening it; or as if the spirits of earth and air and water were things not to antagonize and arouse. . . . The land and all that it bore they treated with consideration; not attempting to improve it, they never desecrated it.

WILLA CATHER FROM DEATH COMES FOR THE ARCHBISHOP

There is a lovely road that runs from Ixopo into the hills. These hills are grass-covered and rolling, and they are lovely beyond any singing of it. The road climbs seven miles into them, to Carisbrooke; and from there, if there is no mist, you look down on one of the fairest valleys of Africa. About you there is grass and bracken and you may hear the forlorn crying of the titihoya, one of the birds of the veld. Below you is the valley of the Umzimkulu, on its journey from the Drakensberg to the sea; and beyond and behind the river, great hill after great hill; and beyond and behind them, the

mountains of Ingeli and East Griqualand.

The grass is rich and matted, you cannot see the soil. It holds the rain and the mist, and they seep into the ground, feeding the streams in every kloof. It is well-tended, and not too many cattle feed upon it; not too many fires burn it, laying bare the soil.

Stand unshod upon it, for the ground is holy, being even as it came from the Creator. Keep it, guard it, care for it, for it keeps men, guards men, cares for men. Destroy it and man is destroyed.

ALAN PATON FROM CRY, THE BELOVED COUNTRY

THIS, FINALLY, IS THE PUNCH LINE OF OUR TWO HUNDRED YEARS ON THE GREAT PLAINS: WE TRAP OUT THE BEAVER, SUBTRACT THE MANDAN, INFECT THE BLACKFEET AND THE HIDATSA AND THE ASSINIBOIN, OVERDOSE THE ARIKARA; CALL THE LAND A DESERT AND HURRY ACROSS IT TO GET TO CALIFORNIA AND OREGON; SUCK UP THE BUFFALO, BONES AND ALL; KILL OFF NATIONS OF ELK AND WOLVES AND CRANES AND PRAIRIE CHICKENS AND PRAIRIE DOGS; DIG UP THE GOLD AND REBURY IT IN VAULTS SOMEPLACE ELSE; RUIN THE SIOUX AND CHEYENNE AND ARAPAHO AND CROW AND KIOWA AND COMANCHE; KILL CRAZY HORSE, KILL SITTING BULL; HARVEST WAVE AFTER WAVE OF IMMIGRANTS' DREAMS AND SEND THE WISED-UP DREAMERS ON THEIR WAY; PLOW THE TOPSOIL UNTIL IT BLOWS TO THE OCEAN; SHIP OUT THE WHEAT, SHIP OUT THE CATTLE; DIG UP THE EARTH ITSELF AND BURN IT IN POWER PLANTS AND SEND THE POWER DOWN THE LINE; DISMISS THE SMALL FARMERS, EMPTY THE LITTLE TOWNS; DRILL THE OIL AND NATURAL GAS AND PIPE IT AWAY; DRY UP THE RIVERS AND SPRINGS, DEEP-DRILL FOR IRRIGATION WATER AS THE AQUIFER RETREATS. AND IN RETURN WE CONDENSE UNIMAGINABLE AMOUNTS OF TREASURE INTO WEAPONS BURIED BENEATH THE LAND WHICH SO MUCH TREASURE CAME FROM— WEAPONS FOR WHICH OUR BEST HOPE MIGHT BE THAT WE WILL SOMEDAY TAKE THEM APART AND THROW THEM AWAY, AND FOR WHICH OUR NEXT-BEST HOPE CERTAINLY IS THAT THEY REMAIN HUMMING AWAY UNDER THE PRAIRIE, ABSORBING FEAR AND MAINTENANCE, UNUSED, FOREVER. —*IAN FRAZIER FROM* GREAT PLAINS

SU'SAN
RESTAURANT
SU'SAN
LOE MELBA
RAMONA
GREAT ZIEGFELD
HARLEM NITE
MIDNITE SHOW EVERY SAT. 25¢ PROSPECT
HARLEM NITE
MORRIS
PROSPECT
THE BIG GAME

THE FIRST LANDING of the white man was the beginning of the end. Often have I heard the story, a never-failing marvel to the three generations who survived it, of the landing on the banks of the Swan River in 1829. In his camp by a little spring called Goordandalup, a wilderness of bush that is now the metropolitan subdivision of Crawley, on the highway of the Mount's Bay Road, Yalgunga lay dozing in the heat of midafternoon. He did not know that it was 1829, or hear the death knell of his people. He knew only that the world was blue and smiling, and the rock holes filling with fish in the incoming tide, and that the sun was good. Suddenly he heard a new sound on the river, a soft continuous sound, and coming closer. He rose to his feet and looked about instinctively for his spears. His women crouched round him, and his children ran to him afraid. Round the bend came an open boat, and the phenomenon of jang-ga, spirits of the dead who had come back as white men, borne upon the waters. Spears were useless. Yalgunga waited. Walking as other men, the strangers stepped ashore and came to him, speaking words that meant nothing. Then one of them put out a hand in greeting. Yalgunga gratefully clasped it in his own, and with his other hand made a gesture to his camp and his spring—they were all he had to offer. That evening he gathered his family, his spears, and all his belongings, and wandered away to the swamp at Goobabbilup, which is now Monger's Lake, never to return to the leafy home and the curve of bush and beach that had been his alone. So easily had the white man won.

DAISY BATES FROM THE PASSING OF THE ABORIGINES

Overpopulation is really the root of all evil.

KONRAD LORENZ

...the gifts of nature and the works of man are only good
or bad as we make good or bad use of them.

Julian Huxley

THROWING A TREE

The two executioners stalk along over the knolls,
Bearing two axes with heavy heads shining and wide,
And a long limp two-handled saw toothed for cutting great boles,
And so they approach the proud tree that bears the death mark on its side.

～

Jackets doffed they swing axes and chop away just above ground,
And the chips fly about and lie white on the moss and fallen leaves;
Till a broad deep gash in the bark is hewn all the way round,
And one of them tries to hook upwards a rope, which at last he achieves.

～

The saw then begins, till the top of the tall giant shivers:
The shivers are seen to grow greater at each cut than before:
They edge out the saw, tug the rope; but the tree only quivers,
And kneeling and sawing again, they step back to try pulling once more.

～

Then, lastly, the living mast sways, further sways: with a shout
Job and Ike rush aside. Reached the end of its long staying powers
The tree crashes downward: it shakes all its neighbours throughout,
And two hundred years' steady growth has been ended in less than two hours.

THOMAS HARDY

I DID NOT FIND THE WORLD DESOLATE WHEN I ENTERED IT;
MY FATHER PLANTED FOR ME BEFORE I WAS BORN:
SO DO I PLANT FOR THOSE WHO WILL COME AFTER ME.

JERUSALEM TALMUD: TA'ANITH, 23A

Astrov: ... I would consent to cutting wood when people really need it, but why destroy the forest homes of animals and birds are being laid waste, the rivers are getting shallow and drying u lazy and stupid to stoop down and pick up the fuel from the ground... Man given him, but up to the present he's been destroying and not creating. Ther almost exterminated, the climate is being ruined, and the land is getting poore planted with my own hands, I'm conscious of the fact that the climate is t years' time, I'll be responsible for it even though only to a ver green and swaying in the wind, my heart fills with pride.

he Russian forests are literally groaning under the axe, millions of trees are being destroyed, the
onderful scenery is disappearing forever - and all this is happening just because people are too
ndowed with reason and creative power so that he can increase what has been
re fewer and fewer forests, the rivers are drying up, the wild creatures are
nd more hideous every day... when I hear the rustling of the young trees I
ome extent in my power too, and that if mankind is happy in a thousand
inute extent. When I plant a little birch tree and then see it growing

ANTON CHEKHOV FROM: UNCLE VANYA (ACT 1)

The forest is one big thing; it has people, animals, and plants. There is no point saving the animals if the forest is burned down; there is no point saving the forest if the people and animals who live in it are killed or driven away. The groups trying to save the race of animals cannot win if the people trying to save the forest lose. The Indians cannot win without the support of these groups; but the groups cannot win without the help of the Indians, who know the forest and the animals and can tell what is happening to them. No one of us is strong enough to win alone; together we can be strong enough to win.

Fred Pearce quoting Chief Paulinho Paiakan of the Kayapo Indians from Green Warriors

We are saying that the unnumbered phenomena that we see existing in an intricate complex maintain a marvelous degree of order and balance. They melt into one another. They are one another. A cow standing there in the field with its huge wet nose looks singular enough.

What are we saying when we speak of the Order of Nature?

But where does the substance of that heavy piece of flesh it carries come from? The cow is not created out of nothing, it is not really on its own, it is simply part of the universe, a moving part. There is the field: it happens to be stationary. The cow moves about, but it is part of the field, and is continually recruited from the field. It cannot move, it cannot grow, unless it takes in a portion of the field. This is called eating. If it fails to do so, then it will stop in its path, and will sink back into the field. This is called dying.

JOHN STEWART COLLIS FROM THE TRIUMPH OF THE TREE

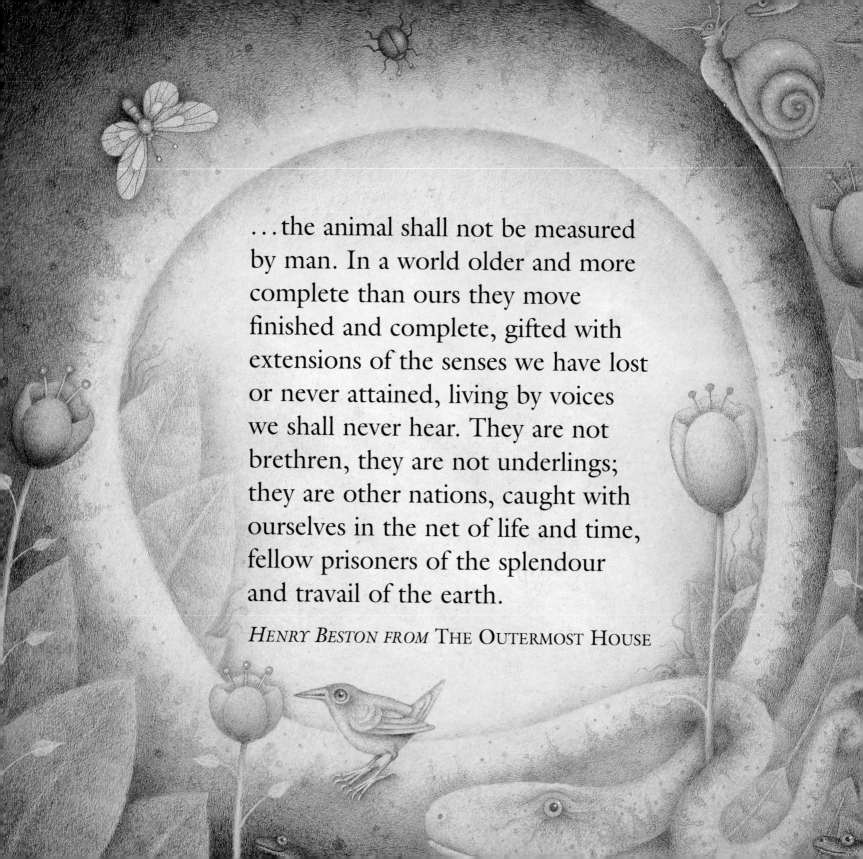

…the animal shall not be measured
by man. In a world older and more
complete than ours they move
finished and complete, gifted with
extensions of the senses we have lost
or never attained, living by voices
we shall never hear. They are not
brethren, they are not underlings;
they are other nations, caught with
ourselves in the net of life and time,
fellow prisoners of the splendour
and travail of the earth.

HENRY BESTON FROM THE OUTERMOST HOUSE

Let the ox proceed with his plowing, or blame his death on advancing years: let the sheep supply us with a defence against the biting north wind, and well-fed goats present their udders to be milked. Away with nets and snares, traps and cunning ruses. Cease to trick birds with limed twigs, to make a sport of hunting stags with feather-decked cords, or hiding barbed hooks beneath your treacherous bait. Destroy creatures that harm you, but even in their case, be content to destroy. Do not let their flesh pass your lips; live on some less barbarous diet.

OVID FROM "THE TEACHINGS OF PYTHAGORAS," THE METAMORPHOSES

THE COMBE

The Combe was ever dark, ancient and dark.
Its mouth is stopped with bramble, thorn, and briar;
And no one scrambles over the sliding chalk
By beech and yew and perishing juniper
Down the half precipices of its sides, with roots
And rabbit holes for steps. The sun of Winter,
The moon of Summer, and all the singing birds
Except the missel-thrush that loves juniper,
Are quite shut out. But far more ancient and dark
The Combe looks since they killed the badger there,
Dug him out and gave him to the hounds,
That most ancient Briton of English beasts.

EDWARD THOMAS

THE HUNTSMAN

Hi! Handsome hunting man
Fire your little gun.
Bang! Now the animal
Is dead and dumb and done
Never more to peep again, creep again, leap again,
Eat or sleep or drink again, oh what fun.

WALTER DE LA MARE

52

LUKANNON

This is the great deep-sea song that all the St. Paul seals sing when they are heading back to their beaches in the summer. It is a sort of very sad seal National Anthem.

RUDYARD KIPLING

I met my mates in the morning (and oh, but I am old!)
Where roaring on the ledges the summer ground-swell rolled;
I heard them lift the chorus that drowned the breakers' song—
The Beaches of Lukannon—two million voices strong!

The song of pleasant stations beside the salt lagoons,
The song of blowing squadrons that shuffled down the dunes,
The song of midnight dances that churned the sea to flame—
The Beaches of Lukannon—before the sealers came!

I met my mates in the morning (I'll never meet them more!);
They came and went in legions that darkened all the shore.
And through the foam-flecked offing as far as voice could reach
We hailed the landing-parties and we sang them up the beach.

The Beaches of Lukannon - the winter-wheat so tall -
The dripping, crinkled lichens, and the sea-fog drenching all!
The platforms of our playground, all shining smooth and worn!
The Beaches of Lukannon - the home where we were born!

I meet my mates in the morning, a broken, scattered band.
Men shoot us in the water and club us on the land;
Men drive us to the Salt House like silly sheep and tame,
And still we sing Lukannon - before the sealers came.

Wheel down, wheel down to southward! Oh, Gooverooska, go!
And tell the Deep-Sea Viceroys the story of our woe;
Ere, empty as the shark's egg the tempest flings ashore,
The Beaches of Lukannon shall know their sons no more!

WE HAVE NEVER UNDERSTOOD
WHY MEN MOUNT THE HEADS OF ANIMALS AND HANG THEM UP TO LOOK DOWN ON THEIR CONQUERORS.

Possibly it feels good to these men to be superior to animals, but it does seem that if they were sure of it they would not have to prove it. Often a man who is afraid must constantly demonstrate his courage and, in the case of the hunter, must keep a tangible record of his courage. For ourselves, we have had mounted in a small hardwood plaque one perfect borrego [long-horned sheep] dropping. And where another man can say, "There was an animal, but because I am greater than he, he is dead and I am alive, and there is his head to prove it," we can say, "There was an animal, and for all we know there still is and here is the proof of it. He was very healthy when we last heard of him."

JOHN STEINBECK & ED RICKETTS FROM THE LOG FROM THE SEA OF CORTEZ

BEFORE I LEARNED TO RESPECT RATTLESNAKES, I KILLED TWO....

I felt degraded by the killing business, further from heaven, and I made up my mind to be at least as fair and charitable as the snakes themselves, and to kill no more save in self-defence.

Since then I have seen perhaps a hundred or more in these mountains, but I have never intentionally disturbed them, nor have they disturbed me to any great extent, even by accident, though in danger of being stepped on. . . . Once—in making my way through a particularly tedious tangle of buckthorn—I parted the branches on the side of an open spot and threw my bundle of bread into it; and when, with my arms free, I was pushing through after it, I saw a small rattlesnake dragging his tail from beneath my bundle. When he caught sight of me he eyed me angrily, and with an air of righteous indignation seemed to be asking why I had thrown that stuff on him. He was so small that I was inclined to slight him, but he struck out SO angrily that I drew back and approached the opening from the other side. But he had been listening, and when I looked through the brush I found him confronting me, still with a come-in-if-you-dare expression. In vain I tried to explain that I only wanted my bread; he stoutly held the ground in front of it; so I went back a dozen rods and kept still for half an hour, and when I returned he was gone.

—JOHN MUIR FROM THE ANIMALS OF THE YOSEMITE

Whenever I injure life of any sort, I must be quite clear whether it is necessary. Beyond the unavoidable I must never go - not even with what seems insignificant. The farmer who has mown down a thousand flowers in his meadow as fodder for his cows, must be careful on his way home not to strike off in wanton pastime the head of a single flower by the roadside, for he thereby commits a wrong against life without being under the pressure of necessity.

By the very fact that animals have been subjected to experiments, and have by their pain won such valuable results for suffering humanity, a new and special relation of solidarity has been established between them and us. From that springs for each one of us a compulsion to do to every animal all the good we possibly can. By helping an insect when it is in difficulties, I am only attempting to cancel part of man's ever new debt to the animal world.

ALBERT SCHWEITZER FROM: CIVILIZATION AND ETHICS

They shall not hurt nor destroy in all my holy mountain. ISAIAH 11, 9

BIRDFOOT'S GRAMPA

The old man
must have stopped our car
two dozen times to climb out
and gather into his hands
the small toads blinded
by our light and leaping,
live drops of rain.

The rain was falling,
a mist about his white hair
and I kept saying

you can't save them all,
accept it, get back in
we've got places to go.

But, leathery hands full
of wet brown life,
knee deep in the summer
roadside grass,
he just smiled and said
they have places to go, too.

JOSEPH BRUCHAC

60

In February 1984 a panda that had fallen into a partially iced-over river and found itself in difficulties was rescued by three girls out collecting firewood. They jumped into the freezing water to save it, and then lit a fire to dry it off while other peasants brought bamboo branches, boiled rice, meat, and sugar on which it fed before returning to the forest.

DAVID TAYLOR FROM
THE GIANT PANDA

One spring day a hunter shot at a flight of wild swans
and brought down the leader. By chance it fell at the feet of
the young Buddha. He soothed the bird, withdrew the arrow
and laid cool leaves and healing honey on the wound.
When the hunter claimed his prey, Buddha refused to part
with the swan. His decision was supported by an unknown priest
who argued that a living thing belongs more to him who
preserves its life than to him who tries to destroy it.
"The Slayer spoils and wastes, the cherisher sustains;
give him the bird."
With that, the unknown priest mysteriously disappeared
and Buddha released the swan, fully healed,
to rejoin its kind.

RETOLD FROM: SIR E ARNOLD, THE LIGHT OF ASIA

In China, every autumn, farmers build little huts out of straw — to house hibernating spiders beside the paddy fields. The Chinese were the first to use spiders in the control of

pests; by protecting them in little huts, the spiders survive the winter and are ready early in the spring to attack the hordes of insects which damage the crops.

PAUL HILLYARD FROM: THE BOOK OF THE SPIDER

All the frustrations involved in releasing animals to the wild are more than made up for when you join forces with people and meet with success, as in the case of the Golden lion tamarins.

Naturally, a plan of this magnitude had to be approached with great caution and attention to detail. An ecological survey had to be done to assess the wild population of Golden lions and, this done, to locate an area of forest uninhabited by a wild population but suitable for the release of the captive-bred specimens. . . . An animal which is perhaps the third generation born in captivity is used to set mealtimes and never has to go out and search for its food. Most important of all in the cushioned world of captivity, there are no predators in the shape of snakes and hawks, and even *Homo sapiens* is considered an obliging gift-giving friend. So the animals have to be introduced slowly to the stern realities of life in the forest if they are to survive. At one point it was discovered that they were alarmed and daunted by tree branches which bent. In the well-conducted zoos they came from the branches were rigidly nailed into place, so a branch which gave under your weight was an alarming experience until you learnt how to cope with it. They had to learn to incorporate into their diets wild fruit they had never seen before and here it was discovered, fascinatingly enough, that the younger animals were quicker at learning this and were showing the older ones what to do.

The initial releases got off to a slow start, but as the animals *and* the people in charge of the project learnt more and more they were finally successful. One photograph shows a captive-bred specimen eating a frog, an item never included in her diet in Washington, and proof that the animals had settled down in their environment. The next phase involved releasing captive-bred animals with wild ones, and it was a great day when twins were produced by a female born in captivity but who had mated with a male born in the wild. By this time we had bred over twenty-five Golden lions in Jersey and so were able to take part in the venture by donating five of our animals. They were released as a family group in a patch of forest with no wild tamarins present, and we're very proud to say that our group was the first in the project to produce offspring from parents which had *both* been born and raised in captivity. This is proof, if proof were needed, that if all the various disciplines involved work in harmony towards a common goal, captive breeding can and does work, and with it we should be able to pull back innumerable species from the brink of extinction.

GERALD DURRELL FROM THE ARK'S ANNIVERSARY

68

It was Serozha's birthday, and he received many different gifts—peg-tops and hobby-horses and pictures. But Serozha's uncle gave him a gift which he prized above all the rest: it was a trap for snaring birds. The trap was constructed in such a way that a board was fitted on the frame and shut down upon the top. If seed were scattered on the board, and it was put out in the yard, the little bird would fly down, hop upon the board, the board would give way, and the trap would shut with a clap.

Serozha was delighted and he ran to his mother to show her the trap.

His mother said, "It is not a good plaything. What do you want to do with birds? Why do you want to torture them?"

"I am going to put them in a cage. They will sing, and I will feed them."

Serozha got some seed, scattered it on the board, and set the trap in the garden. And he stood by and expected the birds to fly down. But the birds were afraid of him and did not come near the cage. Serozha ran in to get something to eat and left the cage.

After dinner he went to look at it; the cage had shut, and in it a little bird was beating against the bars.

Serozha was delighted, took up the bird, and carried it into the house.

"Mamma, I have caught a bird; I think it is a nightingale; and how its heart beats!"

His mother said it was a canary. "Be careful! don't hurt him; you would better let him go."

"No; I am going to give him something to eat and drink."

Serozha put the canary in a cage, and for two days gave him seed and water and cleaned the cage. But on the third day he forgot all about the canary, and did not change the water.

And his mother said, "See here; you have forgotten your bird; you would better let him go."

"No; I will not forget him again; I will immediately give him fresh water and clean his cage."

Serozha thrust his hand into the cage and began to clean it, but the little bird was frightened and fluttered. After Serozha had cleaned the cage, he went to get some water. His mother perceived that he had forgotten to shut the cage door, and she called after him, "Serozha, shut up your cage, else your bird will fly out and hurt himself."

She had hardly spoken these words, when the bird found the door, was delighted, spread his wings, and flew around the room toward the window. But he did not see the glass, and struck against it and fell back on the window-sill. Serozha came running in, picked up the bird, and put it back in the cage. The bird was still alive, but it lay on its breast, with its wings spread out, and breathed heavily. Serozha looked and looked, and began to cry, "Mamma, what can I do now?"

"You can do nothing now."

Serozha did not leave the cage all day, but gazed at the canary, and all the time the bird lay on its breast and breathed hard and fast.

When Serozha went to bed, the bird was dead. Serozha could not get to sleep for a long time; every time that he shut his eyes he seemed to see the bird still lying and sighing.

In the morning, when Serozha went to his cage, he saw the bird lying on his back, with his legs crossed, and all stiff.

After that Serozha never again tried to snare birds.

Leo Tolstoy The Bird

WATCHING A BIRD

I was lying in a deckchair in the garden on a pleasantly warm day when my attention was caught by a bird flying toward a bush. I only saw a flash of it and then it disappeared into the bush. I stood up and walked softly over toward the bush. As I parted the leaves to see the bird I heard a swishing sound. I peered through the leaves and saw a small bird standing on a branch near the edge of a nest. I recognized it as a Robin immediately because of his breast, which was colored red and orange and had a tint of mahogany near the edge, where the red faded away to a light brown with dark lines of black, showing where the wings were tucked away on its back. It had small thin legs colored dark brown and the outer skin looked as though it consisted of a lot of scales, like a fish. The small claws pressed the thin bark and made marks as though someone had stuck a pin in and pulled it out again. The Robin's head was small and it had a small pointed beak. As the few sunbeams leaked through the heavy foliage and alighted on the Robin's soft feathers they shone like a silken cloth. I accidentally knocked my hand against a twig and at the snapping sound the Robin turned his head. It had small beady eyes with a worried watery look in them, as if to say "friend or foe?" Then his beak opened wide and sent forth a sharp piercing high note of danger, which went ringing through my ears.

I saw the Robin's pulse quicken, the trembling legs and the eyes become more watery and worried, and I knew I had been interfering with something I oughtn't to have been. My conscience troubled me, so I let the parted branches come together with a swishing sound and I left the poor frightened bird alone to itself.

BY ALAN (AGED 11)

I was encamped in the woods about a mile back of the rim of Yosemite, beside a stream that falls into the valley by way of Indian Canyon. Nearly every day for weeks I went to the top of the valley, and I was anxious to draw every tree and rock and waterfall. Carlo, a Saint Bernard dog, was my companion–a fine, intelligent fellow that belonged to a hunter, who was compelled to remain all summer on the hot plains, and who loaned him to me for the season for the sake of having him in the mountains, where he would be so much better off. Carlo knew bears through long experience, and he it was who led me to my first interview, though he seemed as much surprised as the bear at my unhunterlike behavior. One morning in June, just as the sunbeams began to stream through the trees, I set out for a day's sketching on the dome; and before we had gone half a mile Carlo snuffed the air and looked cautiously ahead, lowered his bushy tail, drooped his ears, and began to step softly like a cat, turning every few yards and looking me in the face with a telling expression, saying plainly enough, "There is a bear a little way ahead." I walked carefully in the indicated direction, until I approached a small flowery meadow that I was familiar with, then crawled to the foot of a tree on its margin, bearing in mind what I had been told about the shyness of bears. Looking out cautiously over the instep of the tree, I saw a big, burly cinnamon bear about thirty yards off, half erect, his paws resting on the trunk of a fir that had fallen into the meadow, his hips almost buried in grass and flowers. He was listening attentively and trying to catch the scent, showing that in some way he was aware of our approach. I watched his

gestures and tried to make the most of my opportunity to learn what I could about him, fearing he would not stay long. He made a fine picture, standing alert in the sunny garden walled in by the most beautiful firs in the world.

After examining him at leisure, noting the sharp muzzle thrust inquiringly forward, the long shaggy hair on his broad chest, the stiff ears nearly buried in hair, and the slow heavy way in which he moved his head, I foolishly made a rush on him, throwing up my arms and shouting to frighten him, to see him run. He did not mind the demonstration much, only pushed his head farther forward and looked at me sharply, as if asking, "What now? If you want to fight, I'm ready." Then I began to fear that on me would fall the work of running. But I was afraid to run, lest he should be encouraged to pursue me; therefore I held my ground, staring him in the face within a dozen yards or so, putting on as bold a look as I could, and hoping the influence of the human eye would be as great as it is said to be. Under these strained relations the interview seemed to last a long time. Finally, the bear, seeing how still I was, calmly withdrew his huge paws from the log, gave me a piercing look, as if warning me not to follow him, turned, and walked slowly up the middle of the meadow into the forest, stopping every few steps and looking back to make sure that I was not trying to take him at a disadvantage in a rear attack. I was glad to part with him, and I greatly enjoyed the vanishing view as he waded through the lilies and columbines.

JOHN MUIR FROM THE ANIMALS OF THE YOSEMITE

A Doe and Her Three Fawns
Scent Danger

Then, suddenly, the tension was broken. The doe barked urgently and broke away. Behind her a covey of red grouse exploded into the air to come hurtling after her in tight formation on down-curved wings. Shotguns roared as three men with dogs appeared over a rise a hundred yards from the butt. Two grouse faltered in flight, flapped wings broken with No. 5 shot, and fell on a slant; a third towered and crumpled, beak to breast, before pitching down to hit the heather in a cloud of feathers. The rest of the pack whirred close on the heels of the fleeing deer, almost breasting the heather tops, while the spaniels were waved out to collect dead and find wounded.

But one of the springers, seeing the deer, had a mind to chase them and raced after them yelping, while men swore and blew recalls in vain. Heat and high heather soon tired the dog, and he turned when he realized he had no hope of catching the deer. While he sneaked back, to be cuffed and sent out to quest, the deer bounded in headlong flight toward Hoolet Nest with the fawns following in line behind the doe. The ground was new to them, so they ran in her slots. Around dubs of peat, over lichened heather-crowned boulders, across treacherous water channels topped with sphagnum, the waywise doe led her family without faltering. And presently they reached the great sheugh that bordered the rush-grown Hoolet Nest pastures.

The sheugh, or great ditch, deep with sheer peat sides was four feet wide and no obstacle to deer that knew the ground. But in front of it the ground rose to a foot-high bank half as wide as the sheugh. The doe jumped from the bank top, sailed up and over, and touched

down on the far side with three feet to spare. From the spot slotted by her takeoff, Bounce leaped unhesitatingly with forehooves held to his breast and hind legs rigid after the thrust. Landing with inches to spare, he bounded after the doe without slackening pace. Close behind him jumped Dance, who stumbled as she landed. She was on her feet when Skip left the ground. The doe, halting to make sure her fawns were following, saw two running her line, then heard a wild cry from the third; for Skip was in the ditch, having jumped too soon because he thought he had only the bank to clear.

Alarmed, the doe turned back with white flag spread. From the lip of the sheugh she looked down at her fawn, standing neck deep in dark peaty water and wailing piteously, like a hare in a snare or in the grip of a collie's teeth. The fawn leaped at the sight of his mother, furrowing the wet peat with his forehooves; but the ditch was too deep and he fell over backward with his head underwater. Struggling to his feet with much splashing, he coughed the water from his lungs, while the doe, pawing at the top, sent down showers of dry peat that blinded him.

In a panic the doe started to trot along the bank. Skip, afraid she was deserting him, tried to keep pace, plunging and leaping and falling, gulping water when he fell, coughing and drooling when he rose. Peat flinders swirled in the dark cool water; a fat water vole, nibbling at a rush stem on a narrow spit of peat, fled from the disturbance, escaping to its burrow near the top by tracks no deer could follow.

The doe turned where the sheugh was spanned by a little bridge built of turf and birch poles, which was a crossing place used by foxes. Retracing her steps at a smarter pace, she reached her starting place and turned again. And so she carried on, rushing up and down, always turning at the bridge of turf. If she had kept on for a hundred yards she could have gotten the fawn out where the ground was level and the ditch no more than a ribbon of water. But, like a hen confronted with a barrier of netting, she galloped up and down on a short beat, till the fawn in the ditch was exhausted and barely able to keep his head above the water.

Skip was trapped, for he was only a little fawn, twenty inches high at the shoulder, standing helpless in two feet of water with three feet of sheer ditch wall above him. To the August drought he owed his life, for in normal seasons the rains spilled five feet of chill water into the sheugh, and death would have been a matter of seconds. As it was, he was barely able to stand; he was choking and glassy of eye; and his mother was quite unable to help him.

Men and dogs walking toward the bridge of turf with three grouse in the game bag and

two spaniels casting ahead, sent the doe's ears up when she had made her twentieth run along the sheugh. Men were the last things she could have wished for at that moment, yet they were the only beings able to help her fawn. But such understanding was beyond the powers of the doe, who saw in them only additional peril. So she barked, with flag spread full, and trotted away a little distance with Bounce and Dance at her side.

The doe started running in circles as the men approached the sheugh, while Bounce and Dance dropped to the ground in obedience to her gruff bark of command. Skip, wailing heartbrokenly, attracted the dogs, and the dogs, barking their discovery to the men, raced

to the sheugh. In her frenzy of fear the doe cut in closer, till she was running her circle barely sixty yards from the dogs, barking her summons to a fawn who couldn't follow.

John Long, the keeper, wearing a braw suit of tweed and a shirt of Cameron tartan, was the first to reach the sheugh. Laying down the game bag, he called off the dogs and coupled them before looking into the ditch. When he lay down on his belly to peer over the edge, the fawn stood still, shilpet and shivering, and too weak to move.

Long called to his shooting companions to hurry and lend a hand, while the dogs, bobbing on their seats, were warned, "Down. Damn ye! Down!"

"A roe kid droonin' in the sheugh," he said when his son Willie arrived with the laird. "If ye tak me by the feet I'll mebbe manage tae fish it oot."

So they held him by the ankles, and lowered him over the edge. Long's shirt and green tweed jacket were plastered with wet peat before he got his hands on the fawn. Skip, almost indifferent to the touch, allowed himself to be pulled by the neck, then grasped by the forelegs. Only when he was hoisted from the ditch, held firmly in John Long's arms, did he strike out with a forefoot in a last despairing struggle. The blow took the keeper on the cheek, bruising the bone and cutting the skin, which bled on the instant.

"Damn!" said Long, hurriedly dropping the fawn. "I should hae kent better!"

"That might have been your eye . . . ," the laird began. "Take care, Willie," he shouted as the boy knelt to grasp the fawn by the legs. But there was no need for care, for Skip was lying on his side, his tongue protruding from the side of his mouth, his lip drawn back from his lower teeth, his breathing a snort, and his mouth oozing water.

"Look at the auld deer," said Willie, pointing to the doe, who was still bounding on her anxious circuit, barking at intervals.

"Well, sir," said Long to the laird, "this beast's aboot loused. Micht as well chap it on the heed noo and be done wi' it. It'll make grand bait for foxes and hoodies."

The laird turned Skip over with his foot, and found the slim body slack. "Leave it to her," he said at last, "then she'll know. You can do what you like with it in the morning."

But Long was stubborn. "As you say, sir," he said, "but if the foxes come on it in the nicht there'll be little mair than bones gin daylight."

The laird, however, was insistent. The doe didn't know her fawn was dead, and the laird, being a man of some imagination and understanding, wanted to leave her to certainty and mourning. Long, who was a remarkable man in many ways, lacked the finer nuances of imagination and thought the laird was being stubborn. His son, quite frankly, thought he was daft, although he didn't say so.

So they left, with the dogs in hand, walking quickly to allow the doe to tryst with her dead.

Yet, if they could have been present half an hour later, they would have witnessed a strange scene when the doe returned to her fawn. Standing over him, she made low noises in her throat, then gently licked his soaking muzzle. Twice she snorted in his face, all the while tapping him lightly with a caressing polished forehoof, as if bidding him rise and follow. And if they had been present later still, they would have seen her, as Kyack saw her, when she entered Hoolet Nest pines with three fawns at foot.

DAVID STEPHEN FROM SIX-POINTER BUCK

TIGER

"There is a tiger," the villagers told each other. "Out beyond the rice fields, out beyond the swamp, somewhere in the oak woods near the river bank, there is a tiger."

No one was sure where the rumor had started, but it was a strong one, and most people believed it. They began to discuss the best, and safest, way to kill the tiger.

"But why kill it?" said Lee, who was the youngest of the children if you didn't count the babies.

"Because if you eat the meat of a tiger," said his uncle, "you yourself become as brave as the tiger. Which is why it's a bad idea to poison it."

"Also, its skin can be sold for an enormous amount of money," said his father. "Which is why it's a bad idea to set metal traps. They might damage it and lower the value."

"Lee," said his uncle, "you must never tell anyone outside the village what we're planning. It's against the law to sell a tiger skin, and we could go to jail."

"I'll never tell," said Lee.

Later, he asked his mother if eating tiger meat really made you brave.

"You're as brave as you think you are," said his mother. "Eating a rose petal will make you brave—if you believe it will."

Lee looked out over the fields toward the swamp and the oak woods beyond.

"I don't want them to kill it," he said.

"It's probably just a story," said his mother. "It probably isn't there at all."

"It is there," said Lee. "I know it is."

A few days after the tiger rumor, another rumor started. The new one was about a great hunter who was traveling in the direction of the village.

"That's handy," said Lee's uncle.

"We'll have to pay him," objected Lee's father.

"Better to get the tiger and give away some of the profit than to go after it ourselves and fail—or be killed," said Lee's uncle.

Not long after the rumor, the hunter himself arrived.

He ate the food they offered. He listened while they told him about the magical meat and the money to be made from the skin, and then he got ready to begin. Several men offered to go with him to help dig a pit for the tiger to fall into or to carry the carcass home, but he refused them.

"To find the tiger," he said, "I need to travel quietly and alone."

"Good hunting," said the villagers—all but one.

"Bad hunting," said Lee. "I hope it gets away."

The hunter stared at Lee.

Lee stood straight and stared back.

The hunter turned and walked out of the village.

"How will he kill it?" whispered Lee's uncle as he went.

"Shoot it," said Lee's father. "I think I saw a gun in his pack with a telephoto lens, so he doesn't have to get too close."

By early evening the hunter was walking slowly by the edge of the oak woods, near the river. Every now and then, he saw the footprints of a large animal in the damp earth of the riverbank.

"Pug marks," said the hunter to himself, moving ever more slowly, ever more quietly.

After a time he came to a clearing. An animal lay in the clearing, a deer. It was dead and had been partly eaten.

The hunter sat down beside a tangled bush and waited. Behind him a tree rustled. There was a sound like a rug being shaken in the wind, and then a huge bird flopped down onto the deer and stabbed at it with its beak. Another followed.

But before the second vulture could start to eat, something burst out of the long grass at the edge of the trees and ran at the birds. It was a big golden cat with dark markings that were so like the shadows of branches and grass stems that it had been invisible until it moved.

"Tiger," whispered the hunter to himself.

The first vulture flapped clumsily into the air. The tiger cuffed the second, slower bird with its great paw. Then it got a firm grip on its prey with its jaws and dragged it back under the shelter of the oak where it had been dozing.

"A fine male," said the hunter to himself. "Fully grown, but young."

The tiger began to eat the rest of the meat.

"I must try to get a shot from here," thought the hunter, "but the angle is difficult and the tree is in the way."

He moved very cautiously, very gently, but the tiger's sharp ears caught the sound. It raised its head, showed its teeth in a silent snarl—and was gone.

"That was a foolish mistake," thought the hunter. "I must be more careful."

He waited through the night. At dawn he sought out the fresh trail and began to follow it.

It was two days before he saw the tiger again.

By the light of the evening sun, he watched it sharpening its claws on the bark of a tree, stretching its full length against the trunk. He got it in his sights, but at the last second, even though it didn't hear him, didn't see him, the tiger moved and spoiled his shot.

At dusk he watched it washing its golden striped fur with great sweeps of its rough tongue.

"I can't take you now," thought the hunter. "The light is bad, and the shadows make it hard to judge the distance."

That night he watched it stalk another deer, creeping so slowly through the undergrowth that sometimes it didn't seem to move at all for almost ten minutes.

"You are as patient as I am," thought the hunter.
He watched it make its leap. He watched the
deer spring away and the tiger go for its
hindquarters and miss. The deer ran.
The tiger didn't chase it. All its power
had gone into the first attack.

"You probably always miss more
than you catch," the hunter
thought. "But it doesn't
matter. You're sleek
and well fed."

The next day, in the heat of the afternoon, he watched the tiger drink from the river, and then fling itself into the water with a great splash, and swim strongly downstream, just for the cool pleasure of it.

That was when he got his first clear shot, as the water streamed off the tiger's head, and its body undulated just below the surface.

The tiger saw him. It clambered out of the water and shook like a dog, sending drops sparkling all around. That was when the hunter got his second shot.

The tiger faced him.

"You're no man-eater," said the hunter, "You with your sharp teeth and strong bones—you live on wild deer and wild pig. You won't go for me."

And he got the fine head and great chest right in his sights and took the third shot.

The tiger snarled to warn him not to come any closer, but it did not attempt to attack him. It turned its back and loped elegantly away and out of sight, in among the oak trees.

The hunter packed away his camera and rested for a while before beginning the trek back to the village.

When he returned, the villagers hurried to meet him.

"Do you need us now, to carry him back?" said Lee's father.

"I'm sorry," said the hunter, "not to bring the news you want, but I'm afraid there's nothing to carry back."

"But there is a tiger out there?" said Lee's uncle.

"I am the best tracker and the best hunter in the region," said the hunter. "If there were a tiger, I would have seen him."

"Do you mean you *didn't* see a tiger?" said Lee's uncle.

The hunter stared at him. Lee's uncle began to fidget.

"Are you trying to pick a fight with me?" said the hunter.

"No," said Lee's uncle quickly, remembering that he had never eaten tiger meat in his life.

"You're very wise," said the hunter, who had never eaten it either. "I'll be on my way, then."

"So it was only a rumor," sighed the villagers, and they shrugged off their disappointment and returned to work.

As the hunter passed by, Lee stepped out in front of him. "There is a tiger, isn't there?" he said. "I know there is—but I'll never tell."

The hunter stared down at him. Then he smiled. Then he winked. Then he continued on his way.

Out in the grassy clearing, beyond the rice fields, beyond the swamp, behind the oak woods, the tiger rested on his back in the shade, one fat paw drooping comfortably onto his white chest.

JUDY ALLEN

THINKING LIKE A MOUNTAIN

A deep chesty bawl echoes from rimrock to rimrock, rolls down the mountain, and fades into the far blackness of the night. It is an outburst of wild defiant sorrow and of contempt for all the adversities of the world.

Every living thing (and perhaps many a dead one as well) pays heed to that call. To the deer it is a reminder of the way of all flesh, to the pine a forecast of midnight scuffles and of blood upon the snow, to the coyote a promise of gleanings to come, to the cowman a threat of red ink at the bank, to the hunter a challenge of fang against bullet. Yet behind these obvious and immediate hopes and fears there lies a deeper meaning, known only to the mountain itself. Only the mountain has lived long enough to listen objectively to the howl of a wolf.

Those unable to decipher the hidden meaning know nevertheless that it is there, for it is felt in all wolf country, and it distinguishes that country from all other land. It tingles in the spine of all who hear wolves by night, or who scan their tracks by day. Even without sight or sound of wolf, it is implicit in a hundred small events: the midnight whinny of a packhorse, the rattle of rolling rocks, the bound of a fleeing deer, the way shadows lie under the spruces. Only the ineducable tyro can fail to sense the presence or absence of wolves, or the fact that mountains have a secret opinion about them.

My own conviction on this score dates from the day I saw a wolf die. We were eating lunch on a high rimrock, at the foot of which a turbulent river elbowed its way. We saw what we thought was a doe fording the torrent, her breast awash in white water. When she climbed the bank toward us and shook out her tail, we realized our error: it was a wolf. A half-dozen others, evidently grown pups, sprang from the willows and all joined in a welcoming melee of wagging tails and playful maulings. What was literally a pile of wolves writhed and tumbled in the center of an open flat at the foot of our rimrock.

In those days we had never heard of passing up a chance to kill a wolf. In a second we were pumping lead into the pack, but with more excitement than accuracy: how to aim a steep downhill shot is always confusing. When our rifles were empty, the old wolf was down, and a pup was dragging a leg into impassable slide-rocks.

We reached the old wolf in time to watch a fierce green fire dying in her eyes. I realized then, and have known ever since, that there was something new to me in those eyes—something known only to her and to the mountain.

I was young then, and full of trigger-itch; I thought that because fewer wolves meant more deer, that no wolves would mean hunters' paradise. But after seeing the green fire die, I sensed that neither the wolf nor the mountain agreed with such a view.

※※※

Since then I have lived to see state after state extirpate its wolves. I have watched the face of many a newly wolfless mountain, and seen the south-facing slopes wrinkle with a maze of new deer trails. I have seen every edible bush and seedling browsed, first to anaemic desuetude, and then to death. I have seen every edible tree defoliated to the height of a saddle horn. Such a mountain looks as if someone had given God a new pruning shears, and forbidden Him all other exercise. In the end the starved bones of the hoped-for deer herd, dead of its own too-much, bleach with the bones of the dead sage, or molder under the high-lined junipers.

I now suspect that just as a deer herd lives in mortal fear of its wolves, so does a mountain live in mortal fear of its deer. And perhaps with better cause, for while a buck pulled down by wolves can be replaced in two or three years, a range pulled down by too many deer may fail of replacement in as many decades.

So also with cows. The cowman who cleans his range of wolves does not realize that he is taking over the wolf's job of trimming the herd to fit the range. He has not learned to think like a mountain. Hence we have dustbowls, and rivers washing the future into the sea.

ALDO LEOPOLD FROM A SAND COUNTY ALMANAC AND SKETCHES HERE AND THERE

*Nature is often hidden,
sometimes overcome,
seldom extinguished.*

FRANCIS BACON

BIOGRAPHIES

AUTHORS WHOSE WORK
APPEARS IN THIS ANTHOLOGY

C. means Contemporary

Douglas Adams. *C.* British author of international bestsellers, including *The Hitchhiker's Guide to the Galaxy.*

Alan. *C.* One of several young writers who contributed to *The Journal of Education* in the mid-1950s.

Judy Allen. *C.* British writer.

Sir Edwin Arnold. 1832–1904. English poet and journalist.

Sir David Attenborough. *C.* British naturalist, writer, and television presenter.

Francis Bacon. 1561–1626. English philosopher and statesman.

Daisy Bates. 1863–1951. Born in Ireland, she lived mostly in Australia, working for Aboriginal welfare.

Henry Beston. 1888–1968. American writer of books about the natural world.

Sir John Betjeman. 1906–1984. British poet. Appointed Poet Laureate in 1972.

John Bierhorst. *C.* American conservationist, writer, and authority on Native American songs and legends.

Joseph Bruchac. *C.* Native American poet and storyteller whose work is based in his own Abernaki culture.

Mark Carwardine. *C.* Zoologist, writer, and photographer.

Willa Cather. 1873–1947. American novelist, poet, and journalist.

Anton Chekhov. 1860–1904. Russian playwright and short-story writer (born in the Ukraine).

John Stewart Collis. 1900–1984. Writer and ecologist, considered one of the pioneers of the ecological movement.

Grandfather David (Monongua). *C.* Chief of the Hopi Nation of North America.

Walter de la Mare. 1873–1956. English poet. Writer of verse, short stories, and novels for adults and children.

Canon Anthony Duncan. *C.* Scottish poet and writer on spirituality and mysticism.

Gerald Durrell. 1925–1994. British naturalist, writer, broadcaster, and founder of Jersey Zoo.

Ian Frazier. *C.* American writer.

James George. *C.* Environmentalist and one-time Canadian Ambassador.

Thomas Hardy. 1840–1928. English novelist and poet.

Paul Hillyard. *C.* Curator of London's Natural History Museum and leading arachnologist.

Sir Julian Huxley. 1887–1975. English biologist and one of the founders of the World Wildlife Fund (now the World Wide Fund for Nature).

Isaiah. 8th century B.C. Old Testament prophet.

Rudyard Kipling. 1865–1936. Indian-born British writer of poetry, novels, and stories for children, including the two *Jungle Books.*

Aldo Leopold. 1886–1948. American conservationist and ecologist.

Konrad Lorenz. 1903–1989. Austrian zoologist, biologist, and one of the founders of the science of ethology (the study of an animal's behavior in its natural habitat).

Kevin McCann. *C.* British writer.

John Muir. 1838–1914. Scottish-born naturalist and environmentalist who lived in California. Considered the father of the environmental movement.

Alice Nannup. *C.* Born in western Australia of an Aboriginal mother and a Caucasian father.

Ovid (Publius Ovidius Naso.) 43 B.C.–A.D. 17. Roman poet.

Chief Paulinho Paiakan. *C.* Head of the Kayapo Indians of the Amazonian rain forest.

Alan Paton. 1903–1988. South African writer and teacher.

Pythagoras. 6th century B.C. Greek philosopher and mathematician.

Ed Ricketts. 1896–1948. Biologist. At one time had his laboratory in Cannery Row, California. Friend of John Steinbeck's.

Albert Schweitzer. 1875–1965. Medical missionary, theologian, musician, philosopher, and winner of the Nobel Peace Prize in 1952.

John Seymour. *C.* Environmentalist and writer who practices what he teaches.

John Steinbeck. 1902–1968. Award-winning American novelist (originally trained as a marine biologist).

David Stephen. 1910–1989. Scottish naturalist, photographer, conservationist, and author.

David Taylor. *C.* Veterinarian who works as a consultant with zoos worldwide.

Edward Thomas. 1878–1917. Poet, biographer, critic. Sometimes wrote under the name Edward Eastaway.

Count Leo Tolstoy. 1828–1910. Russian writer. Author of *War and Peace,* which many consider the greatest novel ever written.

Edward O. Wilson. *C.* Professor of Science and Curator in Entomology at the Museum of Comparative Zoology, Harvard University.

INDEX OF AUTHORS

INDEX OF ILLUSTRATORS

ACKNOWLEDGMENTS

The editor and publishers gratefully acknowledge permission to reprint extracts from the following:

The Living Planet © 1984 by David Attenborough, published by Little, Brown and Company

Asking for the Earth © by James George, published by Element Books Ltd., U.K.

Changing Lifestyles: Living as Though the World Mattered © by John Seymour, published by Victor Gollancz Ltd., London

The Way of the Earth © 1994 by John Bierhorst, published by William Morrow & Company, Inc.

When the Pelican Laughed © by Alice Nannup, Lauren Marsh, and Stephen Kinnane, published 1992 by Fremantle Arts Centre Press, Australia

The Diversity of Life © 1992 by Edward O. Wilson, published by Harvard University Press

Last Chance to See © 1990 by Serious Productions Ltd. and Mark Carwardine, reprinted by permission of Harmony Books, a division of Crown Publishers, Inc.

Death Comes for the Archbishop © 1955 by the Executors of the Estate of Willa Cather, reprinted by permission of Alfred A. Knopf, Inc.

Cry, the Beloved Country © by the Alan Paton Estate, published by Simon & Schuster, Inc.

Great Plains © 1989 by Ian Frazier, reprinted by permission of Farrar, Straus & Giroux, Inc.

The Passing of the Aborigines by Daisy Bates © by John Murray (Publishers) Ltd., London

Essays in Popular Science © by the Julian Huxley Estate, published by Chatto & Windus, London, reprinted by permission of Peters, Fraser and Dunlop

"Uncle Vanya" in *Plays* by Anton Chekhov, translation © 1954 by Elisaveta Fen, published by Penguin Classics, London

Green Warriors © by Fred Pearce, quoting Chief Paulinho Paiakan

The Triumph of the Tree by John Stewart Collis, published by Jonathan Cape, London, reprinted by permission of A.P. Watt Ltd. on behalf of Michael Holroyd

The Outermost House © 1929, 1949, 1956 by Henry Beston © 1977 by Elizabeth C. Beston, reprinted by permission of Henry Holt and Co., Inc.

The Metamorphoses of Ovid, translation © 1955 by Mary M. Innes, published by Penguin Books USA, Inc.

The Log from the Sea of Cortez © 1941 by the John Steinbeck and Ed Ricketts Estates, reprinted by permission of Viking Penguin, a division of Penguin Books USA, Inc.

"The Animals of the Yosemite" in *Wilderness Essays* by John Muir

Civilization and Ethics by Albert Schweitzer, reprinted by permission of Rhena Schweitzer Miller

The Giant Panda © by David Taylor, published by Boxtree, London

The Light of Asia by Sir Edwin Arnold, published by Bauddha Sahitya Sabha, Ceylon, 1944

The Book of the Spider © by Paul Hillyard, published by Hutchinson, London

The Ark's Anniversary © by the Gerald Durrell Estate, published by Arcade Publishing, Inc., a division of Little, Brown and Company

The Long Exile and Other Stories for Children by Leo Tolstoy

Young Writers, Young Readers, published 1960 by Hutchinson, London

"Six-Pointer Buck" © by the David Stephen Estate, published by Lutterworth Press, U.K., in *My Favourite Animal Stories*, collected by Gerald Durrell

Tiger © 1992 by Judy Allen, published by Candlewick Press

A Sand County Almanac and Sketches Here and There by Aldo Leopold © 1949, 1977 by Oxford University Press, Inc.

The editor and publishers gratefully acknowledge permission to reprint the following poems:

"In the Museum of Past Centuries" © by Kevin McCann, from *Green Poetry*, selected by Robert Hull, published 1991 by Wayland, U.K.

"Harvest Hymn" by John Betjeman, from his *Collected Poems* © by John Murray (Publishers) Ltd., London

The Developer © by Canon Anthony Duncan

Throwing a Tree by Thomas Hardy © by Papermac, London

The Huntsman by Walter de la Mare © by the Literary Trustees of Walter de la Mare, represented by the Society of Authors, London

From *The Jungle Book*, "Lukannon" by Rudyard Kipling © by A.P. Watt Ltd., London, on behalf of The National Trust for Places of Historic Interest or Natural Beauty

Birdfoot's Grampa © by Joseph Bruchac, reprinted by permission of Barbara S. Kouts Literary Agent

Photographs reprinted by kind permission of the following agencies:

Andes Press Agency, U.K.
Aspect Picture Library Ltd., U.K.
Barnaby's Picture Library, U.K.
The Bruce Coleman Collection, U.K.
The Hulton Deutsch Collection, U.K.

While every effort has been made to obtain permission, in some cases it has been difficult to trace the copyright holders, and we would like to apologize for any apparent negligence.